ANIMAL BEHAVIOR

Animal
Communication

ANIMAL BEHAVIOR

ANIMAL BEHAVIOR

Animal
Communication

STEPHEN M. TOMECEK

CHELSEA HOUSE
PUBLISHERS
An imprint of Infobase Publishing

Chelsea House
An imprint of Infobase Publishing
132 West 31st Street
New York NY 10001

Library of Congress Cataloging-in-Publication Data

Tomecek, Stephen M.
  Animal communication / Stephen M. Tomecek.
    p. cm. — (Animal behavior)
  Includes bibliographical references and index.
  ISBN 978-1-60413-091-1 (hardcover)
  1. Animal communication. I. Title. II. Series.

  QL776.T66 2009
  591.59—dc22   2008040115

Chelsea House books are available at special discounts when purchased in bulk quantities for businesses, associations, institutions, or sales promotions. Please call our Special Sales Department in New York at (212) 967-8800 or (800) 322-8755.

You can find Chelsea House on the World Wide Web at http://www.chelseahouse.com

Text design by Kerry Casey
Cover design by Ben Peterson

Printed in the United States
Bang FOF 10 9 8 7 6 5 4 3 2 1

This book is printed on acid-free paper.

All links and Web addresses were checked and verified to be correct at the time of publication. Because of the dynamic nature of the Web, some addresses and links may have changed since publication and may no longer be valid.

Cover caption: A male Hamadryas baboon intimidates other males by opening his mouth wide.

Contents

The Basics of Communication

COMMUNICATION IS A MAJOR part of our daily lives. When we pick up the phone to order a pizza, we're communicating. When we text message or e-mail a friend, we're communicating. Even when we yell at family members or cheer on our favorite sports team, we're communicating. In fact, humans do so much communicating, they usually take it for granted. The truth of the matter is that without communication, our lives would be very difficult.

In simple terms, communication is the act of passing or sharing information between individuals. Because we live in a complex society, we depend on communication to help our lives run more smoothly. Try to imagine a typical day if you could not communicate with other people. After waking up, you might be able to get dressed and make it through breakfast. Of course, you would have to find your own clothes and food because you wouldn't be able to ask any questions or get any answers. Once you left home, things would really get interesting. There would be no point in going to school. Without communication, teachers wouldn't be teaching. Staying home would not be much better, though. There would be no television, computer games, or Internet. Books, newspapers, and magazines would be out of the question, too. If you went out to meet your friends, you might never find them because you wouldn't know where they were. If you did happen to stumble across a person you knew, it would be pretty boring. You couldn't talk or make plans.

If it were not for communication, our society would crumble. Think of communication as the "glue" that holds society together.

Communication comes in many forms. All communication involves the use of **signals.** A signal could be a sound, a look, a motion, or even a written sign. Communication also involves different numbers of individuals. When a newscaster on television reports on the day's events, he or she is communicating with many people at one time. When a parent comforts a crying child, or when a coach talks to a player, the communication is one on one.

Humans may be the masters of communication, but we are not the only ones who use it. Every animal, from the smallest insect to a blue whale, uses some type of communication. Humans need communication to get through the day, and so do the rest of the animals on planet Earth. The ability to share information with other living things is an important survival tool.

WHY DO ANIMALS COMMUNICATE?

Although they have different lifestyles than humans, other animals use communication for many of the same reasons. Elephants and insects aren't interested in the latest entertainment gossip or sports scores. Yet, they have the same basic needs as humans. Getting food, staying safe, finding a mate, and protecting territory are some of the things that animals and humans have in common. Communication helps with all of these. What follows are a few of the important reasons that animals communicate.

COMMUNICATION GOES BEYOND SPEAKING

Without a doubt, the most common way that people communicate is through spoken words. Over time, humans have evolved specialized organs for producing and receiving sounds. When it comes to the spoken word, our sense of hearing is the most important. Still, we frequently use all five of our senses to pass information to each other.

Non-verbal communication happens all the time, even if we don't realize it. When you wave to friends, you are saying "hello" even though you never said a word. When baseball players give each other a "high five," they are using the sense of touch to say "well done." When a person uses perfume or cologne, they are sending a message to other people using the sense of smell. When someone offers you a sweet treat to eat, he or she is communicating with your sense of taste. Many other animals use sound to communicate with each other, but they also depend on other senses to send and receive messages.

Identity

All animals must let others know who they are. This is called establishing one's identity. Every living thing on the planet belongs to a **species.** Because there are millions of species on Earth, every animal must be able to recognize his or her own kind. Otherwise, animals would waste time and energy trying to mate with individuals that belong to other species.

Identity is also important for animals that live and work in groups. For a wolf in a pack or a bee in a hive, it is important to clearly belong there. Otherwise, the wolf or bee may be turned away or killed.

Identity is also important for animals who mate for life and who take care of their young. Many mammals and birds are **monogamous.** Just as people recognize their girlfriends, boyfriends, and spouses, other animals have ways of recognizing their mates. This is even more important when it comes to caring for offspring. For example, emperor penguins live in giant groups called rookeries. When parents return with food for their young, they need a way to identify which of the thousands of chicks belongs to them. Otherwise, they might feed a baby that was someone else's.

Mating

One of the most important uses of communication in the animal kingdom happens when animals seek mates. Just about every animal goes through some sort of **courting ritual.** Most often females select mates. To get noticed, males have to "show off" in some way. They use different forms of communication, including song, dance, flashy colors, and acts of strength and bravery. In many cases, successful males will mate with more than one female. The competition between males can be fierce.

Once a female selects a mate, communication comes into play again as the couple decides when to mate. Humans are one of a handful of species that can mate anytime. Most animal species must mate when the female is ready to get pregnant. If a male tries to mate with a female another time, no offspring will be produced. As a result, the females of each animal species have special signals to tell the male it's time to mate. Females use sounds, motions, or changes to the body's scent, shape, or color. However it happens, the way a female expresses she's ready to mate is one of the most important uses of communication in the animal kingdom.

Social Order

Many animals (such as baboons, birds, hippos, and elephants) have distinct social orders in which some individuals are more

An emperor penguin couple huddles over its baby on Dawson-Lambton Glacier in Antarctica. Because emperor penguins have no fixed nest, they use distinct calls to locate their mates and young after they've been separated.

dominant over others. This type of arrangement is called a **hierarchy.** It has many important benefits. Most importantly, it keeps order in the group because members know who the leader

THE ORIGIN OF THE PECKING ORDER

When people use the term *pecking order,* they are referring to where a person ranks in a group. For example, in the army, a general is at the top of the pecking order, followed by a colonel, major, and captain. A private is at the bottom of the pecking order.

The term *pecking order* originated in the 1920s. Scientists noticed that in barnyards, most flocks of hens had a clear hierarchy. One bird dominated another by literally pecking at it. The alpha hen pecked at all the other hens. The "omega" hen, at the bottom of the pecking order, was pecked at by all the other birds. The pecking the birds do is a form of communication. It establishes rank without the birds having to physically fight it out. This saves a great deal of energy and injury.

is. It also enables each member to know where he or she stands in relation to the other animals and what its roles among an animal group may be.

In many cases, one individual dominates the group. Known as the "alpha" individual, this male or female will direct the actions of the other members in the group. In times of crisis, such as when the group has to move in search of food or escape from being attacked by some other animal, group members take their cues from the alpha individual. Below the alpha individual are usually other high-ranking members. They help to keep order over the lower members of the group.

Depending on the type of animal, an individual gets his or her rank in different ways. Sometimes rank is based on age, with the older animals having the higher ranks. Often, especially among male group members, the highest-ranking individuals are the strongest and most able to stand up to the physical challenges of other group members. An alpha individual uses different communication techniques to show that he or she is the "top dog." By communicating his or her alpha status to the others, the alpha animal does not have to constantly fight to stay on top. This not only brings peace to the group, but also saves all the group members a great deal of energy and injury.

Marking Territory Boundaries

Many animals are **territorial.** They feed, nest, and mate in only one area. An animal's territory is important because it has resources that the animal needs to survive. As a form of communication, animals will mark the boundaries of their territories. This is similar to a person putting up a fence around his or her property. Animals use different ways to mark territories but they all communicate the same message to intruders: "Stay out!"

Once a territory has been established, it's up to the individual or members of the group to defend it. Animals will patrol the boundaries of their territory looking for intruders. Usually animals will respect the boundaries set up by other individuals of their own species. However, when food and other resources are in short supply, or if it is mating season, territorial disputes between members of the same species will happen.

If "outsiders" are found within an animal's territory, then the animal will use different warning signals. These basically tell the intruders to "get out" or else there will be trouble. If warning signals don't work, an animal may call out to other members of its group to come and defend the "turf." Animals usually will fight to defend a territory only as a last resort.

Protection

Unless it is a **predator** hunting for food, most animals would rather not fight another animal. Predators are often on the

A black rhinoceros in Tanzania marks its territory by spreading out its urine and dung with its hind feet.

lookout for their next meal. Meanwhile **prey** usually is being careful to avoid becoming someone else's next meal. Many animals that live in groups have specific calls or movements that warn the rest of the group members when a predator is close. These warning signals are critical. They allow the group to run away or to band together and defend itself.

When cornered by a predator, some animals will try to "bluff" their way out of a fight. They might swell up their bodies so that they look bigger. They might show their teeth, claws, or other body parts suggesting to the predator that an attack might result in injury. In some cases, animals will use chemical warfare to avoid getting caught. People know when a skunk has been annoyed. The smell they give off tells the tale.

Finding Food

All animals need food to survive. For many animals, most waking hours are spent in search of the next meal. Animals that live in groups often communicate with one another about the location of food. Calls, body motions, and chemical trails are used by different animal species to signal the location of food.

THE STUDY OF ANIMAL COMMUNICATION

When animals communicate with one another, they follow a certain pattern of behavior. The science that studies animal behavior and communication is called **ethology**. Compared to other sciences, such as astronomy, geology, or chemistry, ethology is a relatively new area of study. The science really started developing in the early 1900s with the work of three outstanding scientists: Konrad Lorenz of Austria, Nikolaas Tinbergen of the Netherlands, and Karl von Frisch, who was born in Austria, but did most of his work in Germany. These three men would go on to win a Nobel Prize in 1973 for their groundbreaking work.

Ethologists look at animals differently from other scientists who study animals. Rather then simply observing how animals behave and what they look like, ethologists focus on *why* animals have certain behaviors and *how* these behaviors have evolved over time.

HOW MODERN SCIENTISTS STUDY ANIMAL COMMUNICATION

Ethology is helping people understand how and why animals communicate and behave the way they do. Scientists working in the field use many of the same methods that were used more than 100 years ago by naturalists such as Charles Darwin. That's be-

Konrad Lorenz, Nikolaas Tinbergen, and Karl von Frisch won the Nobel Prize in Physiology or Medicine in 1973 for their studies about animal communication.

cause these methods are simple: To study an animal in the field, you sit quietly, watch it closely, and record what you see.

Of course, modern field biologists do have certain technological advantages that Darwin didn't have. Darwin had to write down what he saw in a journal. When he wanted pictures, he (or someone else) had to draw them. Modern scientists have computers for taking notes and cameras for taking pictures. They also can use video to record animal motion. Some modern video cameras are so small that they can be attached directly to animals. This gives scientists a true "bird's eye view" of animal behavior. By using global positioning system (GPS) tracking devices and radar, scientists also can see where animals go as they move around their territories or across the globe.

Ethologists today also have sensitive audio equipment to listen to and record the sounds that animals make. By recording the calls and songs of different animals, scientists have been able to detect patterns and slight changes. For many scientists, this information suggests that some animal species use something like a true language.

THE WORK OF LORENZ AND TINBERGEN

Before the development of ethology, scientists called naturalists (people who study natural history) spent a great deal of time observing animal behavior. They rarely asked "why" and "how" animals acted the way they did. That's not to say that naturalists didn't contribute to our understanding of animal behavior. Naturalists such as Charles Darwin and John James Audubon did outstanding work and paved the way for other scientists.

Most of these early naturalists believed that all animal behavior was controlled by **instincts.** An instinct is a behavior that an animal naturally inherits from its parents (in other words, each species has its own set of instincts). This behavior cannot be changed. It can be thought of as an action that is "pre-programmed" and requires no thought. In humans, one instinct is when you jump when startled by a loud noise. Based on the work of Konrad Lorenz and Nikolaas Tinbergen, scientists began to realize that not all behaviors were instincts. In many cases, animals could change behaviors if their environment changed.

Lorenz was born in Austria and was the son of a doctor. He also studied to be a doctor. At an early age, he became interested in the behavior of animals and kept many pets. While working in Germany in the 1930s, he showed that the behaviors of many birds (including ducks and geese) were controlled by the amount of time that young birds spent with their parents. In several cases, he was able to convince young geese that he was their "mother." He did this by removing the chicks from the nest right after they hatched and raising them by hand. The behavior of bonding to a caregiver,

(continues)

(continued)

called **imprinting,** is based on communication that happens between birds and their parents when they are very young.

Tinbergen was born in the Netherlands but did much of his work in England. He established a department of animal behavior at Oxford University. One of his more important contributions to ethology was getting scientists to look at the causes of animal behavior. He showed that understanding the "why" was just as important as knowing what an animal did under different conditions.

While fieldwork still makes up the bulk of studies in animal communication, ethologists also work in laboratories. Scientists called **experimental psychologists** design lab experiments to test how animals communicate. By doing **controlled experiments,** they can learn how animals react to different situations. This gives them a better understanding of how animals learn and why they communicate the way they do.

Other scientists are interested in how animals' brains control communication. The science of **neurobiology** looks at the structure of the brain and the nervous system. One objective is to compare the physical makeup of these systems in other animals to that of humans.

Working individually and in groups, modern ethologists are breaking new ground and unlocking the secrets of animal communication. Their work makes it possible that some day we, too, will be able to "talk" with the animals.

2

Communication Using Visuals

"ACTIONS SPEAK LOUDER than words," according to a popular saying. When it comes to the animal kingdom, sometimes a simple action can speak volumes. Because other animals don't have the same power of speech that humans do, they often rely on actions to communicate. When an animal communicates through movement, scientists call it a **visual display.** Visual displays can covey fear, anger, and the desire to mate. Visual displays also can be used to signal where food is located, if danger is near, or when it's time for a group to move to another location.

Although we depend on speech for most of our communication needs, humans also use visual displays. When a person smiles or frowns, you immediately know how he or she is feeling.

There are differences between the visual displays used by humans and those used by other animals. For one thing, a human display can have more than one meaning. When a person cries, he or she may be feeling fear, sadness, anger, or even extreme joy. To find out why a person is crying, you have to ask. Because animals can't speak the way we do, their visual displays are usually much clearer.

Some visual displays are meant only for members of an animal's own species. These include mating rituals and signals that

A flock of birds takes flight after a dominant bird signals that it's time to go.

tell a group when to move to a new location. Have you ever noticed that when a flock of birds takes off, they often all leave together? It's almost as if one of them said, "Let's go." In fact, this is exactly what happens. The only difference is that instead of using sound, one of the more dominant birds will signal to the rest of the birds using an action called an **intention movement.** In a typical "take off" signal, one bird will raise its wings and lift off the ground a few inches. Seeing this, the birds around it will pick up the signal and pass it to the other members of the group. Within a few seconds, the whole flock lifts off and heads into the sky.

However, not all displays are meant for group members. Some displays can be used to communicate with animals from many different species. One of the most important of these is called a **threat display.**

THREAT DISPLAYS: FIGHT OR FLIGHT

An animal uses a threat display when it feels threatened. The threat could come from a member of its own species, or from a different species. A threat display is a warning. When a dog growls and bares its teeth, it is making a threat display. When bees and wasps swarm around your head after you have accidentally stumbled onto their hive, they are making a threat display. A threat display is an animal's way of saying, "Back off! I don't want to fight you, but if it comes to a fight, I'm prepared to make it a tough one."

In many cases, a threat display can make an animal look tougher than it really is. It's almost a bluff. One example that biologists have recognized involves the so-called "eye spots" on certain moths and butterflies. For example, the Mexican bulls eye silk moth has two large spots on its wings that seem like simple

The Automeris io moth from Ecuador provides a nonverbal threat display, thanks to its bright eyespots.

A cat stalks its prey by slinking along low to the ground until it is ready to pounce.

decorations. Yet, when a predator threatens the moth, the moth brings its wings together so that the spots resemble giant eyes. More often than not, the predator will back off. Scientists are not certain if this display scares the predator into thinking that the moth is larger than it is, or if the patterns of the spots simply startle the predator. Whatever the exact cause, it certainly seems to work.

Threat displays are different from the actions of predators stalking their prey. A hunting animal is in "attack mode" and is clearly the aggressor. For example, cats hunt birds and small animals. When cats are stalking their prey, they stay low to the

BIGGER IS TOUGHER

When an animal uses a threat display, sometimes it's doing more than sending out a warning. The larger an animal is, the more intimidating it is to an opponent. When it comes to bluffing your way out of a fight, bigger is tougher. For example, the arched back and puffed tail of a cat make it appear larger. Cats aren't the only animals that use this type of threat display to ward off an attack. It can be found all over the animal kingdom, from gorillas and bears that stand on their hind legs, to puffer fish and bullfrogs that literally blow themselves up like a balloon.

Humans use a similar visual display when they feel threatened. People will often raise their arms and puff out their chest to make themselves look larger.

A truly unique threat display comes from the sea cucumber. When threatened, these marine invertebrates will push special growths on the inside of their digestive tract out through their anus. These growths not only make the sea cucumber appear much larger, but are also covered in toxic slime. More often than not, the predator will back away.

When threatened, the leopard sea cucumber expels long, sticky, white tubules from its digestive system as a defense.

ground, "slinking" along slowly until they pounce. Their eyes are usually wide open and their ears pointed up. When a cat feels threatened, however, it takes a totally different stance. First, its ears go back. It narrows its eyes to slits. It will then arch its back, and the hair on its back and tail will puff out. Usually, along with this type of visual display, a cat will let out a low growl or hiss. Even without the sounds, you can tell at a glance that the cat is not to be bothered unless you feel like getting scratched.

HIERARCHY SIGNALS

Threat displays aren't always used for defensive purposes. When it comes to animals that live in groups, a type of threat display can be used to show rank. The type of arrangement in which animals are ranked is called a hierarchy. A hierarchy keeps order in the group. Quite often, threat displays are used to assert dominance. When a higher-ranking animal uses a threat display, the lower-ranking animal usually will respond with a **submissive display.** This shows that it knows its place and does not want any conflict.

One example of how signals are used to maintain a group hierarchy can be seen in baboons. When two male baboons "face off," the dominant one will usually close his eyes and yawn. This exposes his sharp canine teeth and white eyelids. Both of these actions signal that he's the boss. In response, a less dominant male will turn his back and hunch over, presenting his rump. While this action might be considered insulting in groups of humans, it is perfectly acceptable to baboons. The submissive male is mimicking the posture of a female who is ready to mate.

DANCING FOR DINNER

All animals need food. For animals that live in groups, finding food is often a cooperative effort. It involves a great deal of com-

A Hamadryas baboon shows its teeth and closes its eyes to let others know that he's dominant.

munication between individuals. Some predators, such as killer whales and wolves, hunt in groups. Working together, they have a better chance of making a kill than if they each hunted alone.

When hunting in an open grassland area, wolves use a hunting strategy that resembles a relay race. When a hunting party comes across a potential victim, the party members usually spread out in an effort to try to cut off the prey animal's escape route. Then one individual (often the alpha member of the party) will start the chase. After a few minutes, a second individual from the group with "fresh legs" will start chasing the prey. This "tag team" approach will continue until the prey is exhausted from running and the group moves in to make the kill.

Hawks usually hunt alone, but they will team up to capture larger prey. Two or three Harris's hawks will fly together until

HUMANS USE SUBMISSIVE SIGNALS, TOO

While social order is different for humans than the rest of the animal kingdom, humans still use signals to show respect. When a judge enters a courtroom, people are expected to stand up. When members of the British royal family enter a room, people bow or kneel. One of the best examples of humans using dominance signals happens within the military. People of lower rank are expected to stand at attention and salute a superior officer. They must hold that pose until the officer returns the salute.

prey, such as a rabbit, is spotted. The birds will then begin to circle and swoop down on the prey from different directions to try to confuse the animal. If the prey is out in the open, the hawks will take turns chasing it until the animal is exhausted. If the prey runs for cover in shrubs and bushes, one or two of the hawks will land on the ground and flap their wings. This "beating" action is designed to flush the prey from its hiding place. When the prey comes out, a circling hawk will pounce on it.

These choreographed "dances of death" involve the use of many signals between members of the hunting party. Without communication, it would be impossible for them to coordinate their attack and come home with dinner.

Although honeybees are not predators, they also work in groups to find food. Instead of hunting parties, bee colonies send out scouts to look for flowers ripe with nectar. When one of these scout bees finds food, she returns to the hive carrying nectar in her stomach and pollen grains on her legs. The scent of the food attracts other bees. Then the scout begins to do a little dance. First translated by Austrian ethologist Karl von Frisch, the act is known as the "waggle dance." This display tells the other bees the direction and distance to the food. After seeing it, other worker bees will go out to collect pollen.

The waggle dance is done in the shape of a figure eight. The scout bee does the dance along the vertical surface of the honeycomb. The dance has three parts. It starts with a circle on one side and then a straight section in the middle, followed by a circle in the opposite direction on the other side. While the bee is moving along the straight section, she will rapidly shake her abdomen back and forth. This is the "waggle" part of the dance.

It turns out that the direction of the straight part of the dance tells the other bees where the food is. If the food is located in the same direction as the sun, the scout bee will move straight

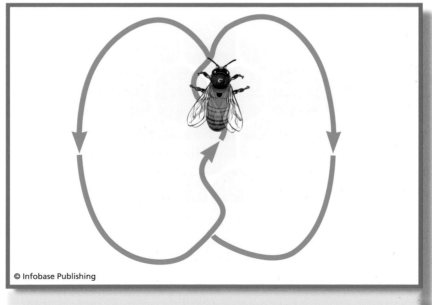

© Infobase Publishing

The figure eight-shaped bee waggle dance is used by scout bees to tell the other bees in their hive the distance and direction to food.

DECODING A BEE'S DANCE

Karl von Frisch first suggested the importance of the waggle dance in the early 1920s. Von Frisch was born in Vienna, Austria in 1886 and received his Ph.D. from the University of Munich in 1910. He began his career studying the behavior of fish by demonstrating how different species would react to different colors. In 1919, he began working with honeybees. He found that bees had a highly developed sense of smell, which helped them find nectar. His biggest breakthrough came when he decoded the "waggle dance."

Other scientists had noticed that bees danced when they returned to the hive, but most never thought of the behavior as a form of communication. After conducting many detailed observations and experiments, von Frisch became convinced that these dancing bees were giving important information to other bees. He worked out the different parts of the dance and presented his ideas to the rest of the scientific community.

At first, many scientists refused to accept the idea that an animal as simple as a bee could handle such complex communication. Most argued that the other bees were simply picking up the odors of the food from the scout bees and using them to find the food. Von Frisch refused to back down. As other scientists tested his idea, they found more evidence to support his claims. For his pioneering work, von Frisch was awarded a Nobel Prize in 1973. Today he is considered to be one of the founding fathers of the science of ethology.

up the honeycomb. If the food is located 30 degrees to the left of the sun, then she will slant the waggle part of the dance so that it is tilted 30 degrees to the left of vertical. If the food is 30 degrees to the right of the sun, then she will waggle 30 degrees to the right of vertical. The distance to the food is shown by how long each cycle of the dance takes place. If the food is close by, say 100 meters or so, then the dance cycle will last less than 2 seconds. If the food is several kilometers away, then the dance is much slower, with each cycle lasting as long as 8 seconds.

MATING DISPLAYS

Finding food is critical for an animal's survival, but the need to mate is almost as important. In the animal kingdom, few forms of communication can rival the displays carried out by animals looking to mate. Both males and females use this type of communication, but more often than not, it's a male who starts the process.

A **mating display** serves several purposes. First and foremost, it is designed to attract a member of the opposite sex. Once a potential mate shows interest, the animal making the display will then "strut his stuff," showing off just how much stronger or how talented he is. If a female likes what she sees, she will usually respond with a display of her own, and the two individuals can mate.

As you might expect, with so many different creatures living in the natural environment, just finding a potential mate can often be difficult. To get around this problem, some animals have evolved special adaptations that help them get the message out. One of the most interesting happens in fireflies. A firefly (also known as a lightning bug) is a type of beetle with a special organ on the underside of its abdomen. This organ produces a yellowish glow called **bioluminescence.** When a male firefly wants to attract a mate, he will begin flashing his light until he receives a light signal from an interested female.

There are more than 1,000 species of fireflies. Each species has its own mating signal, with a unique pattern of flashes. When a female recognizes the pattern for her particular species, she will respond with a similar pattern. The male will then fly to the female and the two will mate.

A firefly flashes light signals to let females know he's ready to mate.

As you might imagine, with lots of males flying around flashing their lights, there is often a great deal of competition to find a female with whom to mate. The faster a male responds to a female's signal, the better his chances of mating. However, there's a drawback to being too quick. It turns out that some species of fireflies eat other fireflies. To attract prey, some female fireflies will use the response code for a different species. When a male flies in thinking he has found a mate, he winds up being a dinner guest with him as the dinner.

BEWARE OF ROADRUNNERS BEARING GIFTS

Often when a man wants to gain the affections of a woman, he will shower her with gifts. It turns out that the roadrunner uses the same approach when he is trying to find a mate.

Roadrunners are flightless birds that live in the desert of the American Southwest. They usually eat things such as small lizards, snakes, and even the occasional scorpion. When a male roadrunner finds a potential mate, he will run up behind her while carrying some type of dead animal in his mouth. He will then start waving his tail back and forth while bowing to her. If that doesn't get her attention, he will start jumping up and down. If she is impressed, she will take the food gift and the two will form a partnership, usually for life. If she's not impressed, she runs away.

This roadrunner carries a precious gift for females in his mouth: a dead lizard.

For many animals, finding a potential mate is only the first step in the mating process. Often, the real action happens when a male tries to convince a female that he is worthy of her affections. Many birds have specific dances that they use to attract females. From the tiny hummingbird to a giant albatross, males have to "strut their stuff" in order to be selected. All of this dancing takes energy. In most cases, the individual who dances the longest is usually the strongest. This is the one that gets chosen by the female.

COMMUNICATING WITH COLORS

Many animals use colors and badges as visual displays for both mating rituals and setting hierarchies. A **badge** is a marking that makes an animal stand out. In general, the bigger or more colorful the badge, the more dominant the individual. A badge can be simple, such as the dark-colored patch on the chest of a male house sparrow. It also can be ornate, such as the feathers of a peacock. In many cases, an animal may not show a badge until it is time to mate or challenge a leader of a group.

Many species of male birds use bright colors to attract mates. Bright colors signal to a female that a male is of high quality. A well-groomed male with brightly colored feathers has a healthy diet with ample food resources. Males that have poor coloration usually have a poor diet. This means that they come from an area where good food may be in short supply. To a female starting a family, this is an important consideration.

COLOR CHANGES FOR LOVE AND WAR

Colors also can be used as signals. When a female baboon is ready to mate, a colored patch on her rump swells and turns a bright red. This is a signal to male baboons that she is in **estrus.** This is the only time that she is fertile and can produce offspring.

If a male **baboon** tries to mate with a female at other times, no offspring would be produced. In this case, a simple color change can save a great deal of wasted effort.

Research shows that female peacocks are first attracted to the sound of male calls. Then they run around the males they prefer in an effort to encourage them to rustle and raise their feathers. This male is about to lift and spread his feathers.

A blue-ringed octopus displays its iridescent blue rings in order to signal that it is ready to attack and release its poison. It can also change the texture of its skin to resemble various backgrounds, including sand and spiky coral.

Color changes can also be used as defensive mechanisms. The blue-ringed octopus lives in the waters of the Pacific Ocean off Australia. Although it is only about 8 inches long, it is also one of the deadliest animals on the planet. It has a gland that releases venom into its saliva. Normally, the octopus is brown or yellow in color. When it feels threatened, however, it will suddenly show tiny blue rings all over its body. The rings signal to those around it that it's about to release venom into the water.

Clearly, visual signals are one of the most important ways that animals communicate with each other. Where there are no spoken words, a dance here and a flash of color there can carry many different meanings.

3

Communication Using Chemicals

LONG BEFORE ANIMALS walked on the land, flew through the air, or swam in the sea, communication was taking place on the Earth. That's because bacteria, one of the simplest life forms, were signaling each other. With no eyes, ears, or nose, how do these single-celled organisms do it? It's simple: They use chemicals.

Bacteria communicate when one cell releases a chemical that is picked up by a receptor on the membrane of another cell. Until recently, scientists didn't really consider this communication, but it is. If the signal sent out by one bacterium causes a change in behavior of another one, then the two are definitely communicating.

Although we rarely think about it, chemicals also play a major role in animal behavior and communication. For example, every scent you smell is really nothing more than a bunch of chemicals. In the animal kingdom, a scent can send messages, especially to members of the same species. Scents can be used to mark a territory, defend the turf, find a mate, and tell other animals where they can find food.

The chemicals that send signals in the animal kingdom are called **pheromones.** That word comes from two Greek words; *pherein,* which means "to transfer," and *hormone,* which means "to excite." The olfactory organs of animals pick up pheromones. These organs usually are found in the nose. As a result, pheromones often are connected to an animal's senses of smell and taste. Pheromones are important communication tools for insects, fish, and most mammals. Birds, however, don't appear to use pheromones.

Pheromones are an easy way for animals of the same species to communicate. Visual displays require a great deal of energy to produce. But pheromones can be made and released with little effort. Pheromones work just as well in the dark as during the day, and they often can last for several hours. Perhaps the most important advantage of pheromones is that the signal they carry is like a code that can be understood only by animals of the same species. Other species, including predators, can't really pick up on what is being "said."

Pheromones do have some drawbacks. It takes time for the scent to travel from one animal to another. Also, unless they are carried by wind or flowing water, pheromones stay where they are put.

Most often, pheromones are created and released by special glands. In some cases, they are mixed with urine or feces.

INSECTS USING INSTINCTS

Pheromones are widely used throughout the animal kingdom. They were first discovered in insects where they play a special role. When insects pick up a pheromone signal, they respond in a pre-programmed way. Insects produce many pheromones; each one triggers a specific response. Scientists have found pheromones that cause insects to mate, mark a territory, send out an alarm, call for an attack, keep working, and lead the way to food.

A great example of how a pheromone works happens with the common silk moth. When she is ready to mate, the female will release a pheromone called bombykol into the air from a

MAN MIMICS MOTH

For humans, understanding insect pheromones can solve problems. Scientists can use insect **pheromones** to trick and trap some annoying pests. For example, gypsy moth larvae can literally chew the leaves off an entire forest of trees. This not only looks bad, but also can ultimately kill the trees. Using a synthetic version of the female gypsy moth pheromone, scientists can lure male gypsy moths into traps. This reduces the gypsy moth population and helps to protect the trees.

Gypsy moth larvae are in the caterpillar stage of life.

gland on her abdomen. When male silk moths detect this chemical, they find the female to mate with her. Male silk moths have feathery antennae with chemical receptors on them. The receptors are so sensitive that a male can pick up a female's signal from more than a mile away. Using his antennae as a guide, the male tracks the female. Bombykol is such a potent pheromone that the amount released by a single female silk moth can stimulate about one billion males. With odds like that, it's fairly certain that if there is a male in the area, the female will be almost guaranteed a mate.

ANTS ON THE TRAIL

Pheromones are also important in social insects such as bees, termites, and ants. A single chemical signal released by the queen can control the actions of the entire colony. Using pheromones, a queen can get drones to mate with her and prevent other females from mating. She can keep all the members of a colony working and have them attack an intruder on command. This last type of action is controlled by something called an alarm pheromone. Anyone who has ever stepped on a nest of fire ants knows just how effective these signals can be.

Sometimes an alarm pheromone can backfire. For example, chimpanzees enjoy snacking on ants. To get the ants out of their nest, a hungry chimp will place a stick in the entrance hole. This usually results in an alarm pheromone being released by individuals that serve as guards at the entrance. Once the message gets to the rest of the colony, the ants begin to swarm the entrance and crawl all over the stick. When the end of the stick is covered with ants, the chimp will remove it and lick them off.

On the subject of food, if you've ever had a picnic outdoors, you've probably noticed lines of ants walking back and

These nomadic African army ants, photographed in Ghana, show how soldier ants form two lines to protect a central lane of ants carrying food.

forth across the ground, the picnic table, or your blanket. The ants are following a trail of pheromones to some food source. Like bees, ant colonies have scouts that look for food. When they find a tasty tidbit, such as a potato chip or a chocolate brownie, they lay down a trail of pheromone back to the nest. Other scout ants then follow the signal back to the food. As they move down the trail, they leave more of the pheromone, so the chemical signal keeps getting stronger. Eventually, the pheromone trail gets so strong that most of the workers find it and follow along, too.

If ants ever find your food, try this: Follow the trail of ants back toward the nest. About half way between the food and the nest, rub your finger across the trail (don't squish any ants). At first the ants will become confused; they will start circling around. That's because you have removed some of the pheromone and broken the trail. Eventually the ants will pick up the signal again and a new trail will develop.

MARKING TERRITORIES

Each animal needs a certain amount of space. This area, known as a **territory,** is the space in which an individual will find food, mate, and carry out most other life functions. The act of selecting, marking, and defending a territory is called **territoriality.**

There are many benefits to having "exclusive rights" to a territory. When food is limited, a set territory rich in resources

TERRITORIAL PETS

Some pet owners have to deal with the territorial nature of their animals. Most mammals, even cats and dogs, have a natural tendency to mark their territories. When you take a dog out for a walk, or let the cat out in the yard, it's very common to see the animal stop every few feet and spray a little urine on a tree, fence, wall, or bush. When other animals of the same species come by later on they get the message. Often, they will mark the same territory.

Unfortunately, sometimes a pet also will decide to mark the territory inside the house, too. This can leave some rather unpleasant odors and do some serious damage to rugs and furniture. The best way to solve this problem is to have the animal spayed or neutered.

THE MUSK DEER'S MISERY

One creature that is paying a high price for having a special scent gland is the Siberian musk deer. This small-ish creature lives in forests throughout China, Mongolia, Siberia, and Korea. The male musk deer is extremely ter-ritorial. Except for mating season, he lives alone. To mark his territory, the male deer rubs his tail against trees and rocks. The chemical substance that comes from the gland near the tail is called musk. Perfume manufactur-ers use musk. It's also a folk medicine used by people living in Asia.

Natural musk is expensive. Musk deer have been heav-ily hunted for their glands. So many musk deer have been killed in recent years that scientists estimate that their pop-ulation has declined by almost half. In 1994, the Siberian musk deer was listed as an endangered species.

makes a meal easy to find. Having a territory reduces the com-petition for food and mates with other individuals of the same species. In many cases, a male that can show a female that he has good territory will successfully find a mate. Of course, the big-gest problem with having a territory is that you have to defend it. This takes time and energy.

To cut down on the number of fights with other mem-bers of the same species, many animals will use chemicals called **scent markers** to mark the boundaries of their terri-tory. These markers work the same way as a person putting up a fence around the property that he or she owns. Most scent markers are powerful and last a long time. Each is unique to the animal that's leaving it.

Frequently, an animal will leave something called a **scent post.** This is a visual display with a pheromone on it. For many animals, pheromones are deposited with either their urine or feces. For example, rabbits and deer will frequently leave a strategically placed pile of feces on a flat rock that marks the boundary of their territory. Male mountain lions will often create a scent post by using their hind legs to kick up a pile of leaves or pine needles. After they have built this visual marker, they leave their scent by urinating on it.

THE BIG RUB

Spraying urine is probably the most common way that a mammal will mark its territory, but it's not the only way it can do it. Many mammals have scent glands located in other parts of their bodies, such as the paws, at the base of the tail, and even in the forehead and behind the ears. Instead of spraying their area with urine, some animals will rub these scent glands on an object.

In many cases, animals also will use scent glands to mark another animal, such as a mate or one of their offspring. This tells the rest of the population to whom that individual "belongs." This behavior can often be seen in house cats. Many people think it's a sign of affection when a cat comes over and starts rubbing its head against them. The cat may like you, but it has another motive. Cats have scent glands all over their faces. When they rub up against you, they are really spreading a chemical message that you belong to them.

MATING MARKERS

Many other animals depend on chemical communication as part of mating rituals. In fact, within the animal kingdom, chemicals often speak louder than words in the language of love.

With the exception of humans, most mammals have an exceptionally good sense of smell. This is because they have a well developed **olfactory system.** This system is made up of receptor cells, which pick up a scent, and nerve cells, which carry a signal to the brain. Mammals also have a specialized section of the brain called the olfactory lobe. This area processes the information sent from the nerve cells. As you might expect, the receptor cells are in the nose of a mammal. When mammals breathe, air passes over the cells that pick up the chemical signals that make the scents.

In addition to having a keen sense of smell, many mammals also have a special structure in their nose called the vomeronasal organ or Jacobson organ. Even though it is in the nose, the Jacobson organ isn't just used for picking up normal scents. This organ also picks up pheromones that are related to mating and sex.

Some male mammals use musk as a pheromone to mark territories. They also use it to signal to females that they are

THE NOSE KNOWS

Many dogs can pick up and follow scents that humans could never detect. Dogs can track lost hikers and sniff out drugs in suitcases because of the number of receptor cells found in their noses. The more scent receptor cells, the better the sense of smell. Most humans have about 5 million receptor cells. A typical dog can have 50 times as many.

When you walk your dog and it suddenly acts strangely, even when no other dog is around, blame it on the nose. Chances are, your dog is picking up scents left behind by another dog, even though you can't smell a thing.

ELEPHANT LOVE POTIONS

When it comes to mating, a male elephant has a unique way of telling whether a female is in estrus or not. The male elephant will follow the female until she urinates. Then he dips the tip of his trunk into the liquid and touches it to the roof of his mouth. This is where his vomeronasal organ is located. If the female elephant is in estrus, a pheromone will send a signal to the male elephant's brain that will cause nitric oxide to be produced in his blood. This chemical stimulates the male elephant, allowing him to mate. If the female is not in estrus, nothing happens.

ready to mate. Young males who are not sexually mature produce very little musk. In general, the more dominant a male is, the stronger the musk. Females tend to prefer dominant males, so the musk helps them make their selections.

Some males attract females by spreading scents in different ways. Often, the musk glands deposit the pheromone in the animal's urine. A male rhinoceros will roll around in his own urine and wear it like cologne. A male hippopotamus will wave his tail back and forth past his anus, where his musk glands are located. This spreads the scent of the musk through the air.

Female mammals also rely on pheromones to alert males when they are ready to mate. Sometimes the chemical is released in the air and sometimes it's mixed with her urine. Either way, when the male picks up the signal, he knows that he has only a short time to act. During a female estrus cycle, males will usually stop everything and concentrate on the act of mating.

Ring-tailed lemurs have special glands near the inside of their wrists that produce smelly secretions. They drag their tail along this area to capture the smell and then wave and vibrate it to give predators a visual and chemical signal to stay away. This ring-tailed lemur is in the defensive position.

CHEMICAL WARFARE AMONG ANIMALS

Many animals use chemicals when they hunt for food. Snakes, scorpions, and wasps all make venom and use it to paralyze their prey. Not all chemicals are used offensively. Many animals use chemical signals to defend themselves. The poison of the blue-ringed octopus is not for hunting. It is strictly a defense mechanism. Other octopi release inky substances when they are frightened. These chemicals act as "smokescreens," confusing attackers.

Skunks have a different way of using chemicals to defend themselves. Skunks are infamous for the stink that they make when they feel they are in danger. Most species have a highly developed scent gland near the anus. This produces a bad-smelling chemical liquid. When a skunk feels threatened, it will do a type of handstand on its front legs, lift its tail, and blast away. An average skunk can project the spray as much as 10 feet (3 meters). Even people who have never been sprayed by a skunk know when one has been in the neighborhood. The smell lingers for days.

Ring-tailed lemurs have an unusual way of using chemicals to settle disputes. A ring-tailed lemur has a long, bushy tail that looks a lot like a feather duster. It uses its tail in "stink fights" with other lemurs. During disputes over mates, a male lemur will use his scent glands to coat his tail with a smelly chemical. Then he holds his tail up over his head, directing the scent toward the face of a competing male. This may not be the most "macho" way to settle a dispute, but it works.

Communication Using Sound

IT'S AMAZING HOW many different animal sounds can be heard in a forest at night. The chirps of crickets, the croaks of frogs, the occasional screech of an owl—animals are using sound to communicate.

There are a number of reasons that sound is such a popular way for animals to communicate. One big advantage is that sound can be used when it's dark as well as during the day. Also, a sound is broadcast in all directions. This means that many animals can receive a message at one time, without having to see who is making the sound. Sounds travel faster than chemical signals. They also travel under water. Even animals that live underground can communicate using sound. To understand how sounds work in animal communication, it is important to first examine what sound is and how it travels.

THE SCIENCE OF SOUND

Sound is a form of mechanical energy. Energy makes things move. Whenever a sound is made, something has to move or vibrate. A **vibration** happens when an object moves back and forth in a regular pattern. When you pluck a string on a guitar or hit a cymbal with a stick, the string or cymbal vibrates and produces sounds. When a person speaks, his or her vocal chords vibrate. When a cricket rubs its legs together and an elephant forces air through its trunk, vibrations occur, too. Every sound that happens in the animal kingdom is the result of something vibrating.

A sound moves out from its source in a series of energy pulses called **sound waves.** These are like the ripples that move across the water after you throw a rock in a pond. The waves on a pond can be large or small, and so can sound waves. The height of a wave is called the **amplitude.** The more energy a sound wave has, the larger its amplitude and the louder the sound.

Scientists measure the intensity or loudness of a sound by a unit called the decibel, or dB for short. As you might expect, sounds made by different animals cover a full range of intensities. They can be very quiet (a cat purring is about 20 dB) or extremely loud (the scream of a howler monkey can reach more than 100 dB). The loudest animal sound reported is the song of the blue whale. It can reach intensities of up to 190 dB.

Amplitude is only one part of a sound wave. Sound waves also can vary in **frequency.** The frequency of a wave describes how many waves pass a point every second. Amplitude controls the loudness of a sound, and frequency controls the pitch. High-pitched sounds, such as those of a small bird chirping, have a high frequency. Low-pitched sounds, such as the roar of a tiger, have a low frequency.

Not only do animals make sounds at different frequencies, but they also hear at different frequencies. The frequency of a sound is measured in **Hertz,** or (Hz). One Hz is equal to one vibration per second. Typically, the human range of hearing goes from about 20,000 Hz all the way down to 20 Hz. Bats can hear sounds that have extremely high frequencies: more than 120,000 Hz. Humans cannot hear these high frequency

Hearing Range of Animals	
Porpoises, bats, and even mice have much better hearing than humans. Here's how people stack up:	
Animal	**Normal Hearing Range (Hz)**
Porpoise	75 – 150,000
Bat	1,000 – 120,000
Mouse	1,000 – 91,000
Cat	60 – 65,000
Cow	25 – 35,000
Dog	15 – 50,000
Human	20 – 20,000

sounds, but bats and other animals use them for communication all the time.

SOUNDS IN THE AIR AND UNDER THE WATER

Sound and light both travel in waves. Light waves can travel through a vacuum, but sound waves cannot. Most often, when we hear a sound, the wave has traveled through the air. Sound also can travel through liquids, including water. In fact, sound travels better under water than through the air. A typical sound travels through the air at about 1,170 feet/second (340 meters/second); in water, it moves about four times faster.

Because water is so much better at transmitting sound waves than air, many sea creatures rely on it for long-distance communication. Using a network of underwater microphones, scientists have been able to pick up sounds made by minke whales swimming more than 100 miles (160 km) away. Humpback whale

This Inuit researcher is using a hydrophone in order to record narwhal vocalization under the arctic ice in Baffin Island, Canada. Narwhals are porpoises found in Arctic coastal waters.

songs can travel even farther: more than 300 miles (500 km). The top honors for underwater communication goes to the two largest species of whales. Blue and finback whales have had songs travel more than 1,500 miles (2,500 km).

Many things affect the travel of a sound wave. In a forest, leaves can deflect and absorb sound waves. This makes it hard for sounds to travel very far. In the ocean, the temperature and salinity of water will affect how a sound wave travels. At a depth of about 3,000 feet (925 m), there is a layer of water that scientists call the SOFAR channel. This stands for SOund Fixing And

Ranging. This layer acts like a tube that carries low-frequency sounds through the ocean for hundreds, and even thousands, of miles. Both blue whales and finback whales use this SOFAR channel to their advantage.

In the air, temperature and weather conditions influence how far a sound wave will travel. When the temperature drops at

INFRASOUND AND ULTRASOUND

Animals can hear and make sounds that we can't hear. Infrasonic vibrations, or **infrasound,** have frequencies below 20 Hz. Because we can't hear them, scientists didn't know until recently that animals made these sounds. In the early 1980s, ethologist Katy Payne was working with elephants at a zoo in Portland, Oregon. She felt some unusual

(continues)

African elephants are among those animals that communicate with sounds humans can't hear.

(continued)

vibrations in her chest. She suspected that the elephants were the source. Using a high-tech device called a sound spectrograph, Payne recorded and analyzed the silent signals that were produced by the animals. She discovered that elephants use infrasound to communicate with each other. As it turns out, so do hippos and giraffes.

Ultrasonic vibrations, or **ultrasound,** have frequencies above 20,000 Hz. Many animals—including bats, porpoises, and rats—use ultrasound to communicate. Some animals, such as dolphins and killer whales, use both infrasound and ultrasound. Because these sounds are outside the normal range of most other sounds, they are easier to detect. In many cases, different animal species will use different bands of sound frequencies for communicating. It's almost like pairs of people talking on different channels on walkie-talkies. If each pair stays on a different channel, their conversations are less likely to be interrupted.

night, sound waves usually will travel father than they do in the middle of the day. In jungles and rain forests, there are more animal calls at dawn and dusk. Both daytime (diurnal) and nighttime (nocturnal) creatures are helped by the natural conditions that maximize the distance in their calls.

ANGER MANAGEMENT AND ALARM CALLS

An animal will often use a visual threat to ward off a predator or avoid a fight with another individual. For many animals, a threat signal wouldn't be complete without an appropriate sound to go along with it. The hiss of a cat, the growl of a dog, and the roar of a lion let opponents know that they are angry and mean business. Angry elephants flare their ears and wave their trunks while trumpeting. The trumpet is the final warning signal before they charge.

Many animals that live in groups have a special type of threat signal that works as a distress call. These **alarm calls** are designed to alert the other members of the group to danger. They can also be a cry for help. Group members take different action when they hear different alarm calls. Sometimes they band together in defensive formations. Other times, they go on the attack. In many cases, when group members hear an alarm call, they simply move away from the source of danger.

Most **vertebrates** use some type of alarm call. The signals used by **primates** are by far the most complex. An excellent example can be found in vervet monkeys, which live in the grasslands and wooded areas along rivers in East Africa. Vervets live in family groups that range from about 20 to 60 individuals. Their main predators are pythons, leopards, and eagles.

Scientists who recorded sounds made by vervet monkeys discovered that they use a different alarm call for each of their three main predators. Even more interesting was the fact that each call provoked a different reaction. If one vervet gave the call for a snake, group members would all stand up and look around. When the leopard call was given, they would climb the nearest tree. When the eagle call was given, they would head for the high grass. To show that the calls had real meaning, the scientists played tape recordings of the alarm calls where vervets could hear them. Sure enough, the monkeys reacted the same way, just as if a group member had given them the signals.

TURF WARS

Many animals also use sounds to gain and defend their territories. The North American woodchuck uses a series of high-frequency whistles when another woodchuck has entered its territory. Scientists believe that male whales use low-frequency sounds to warn other males when they get too close.

When it comes to declaring their territory, few animals can compete with the red howler monkey. These monkeys live in the South American rainforests in family groups called troops. One troop includes anywhere from three to nine monkeys. In the early dawn hours, the dominant males of each troop begin to shriek. This sets off a chorus of other howler monkeys all over the forest. These animals make one of the loudest calls in the animal kingdom; it can be heard more than two miles

A Bolivian red howler monkey sits high in the forest canopy. Its loud calls are amplified as air is forced through a special bone in its throat.

SINGING FOR THEIR HOME

Each spring in North America, the early morning hours are filled with the sweet sounds of songbirds, such as sparrows and robins. While it may seem like these birds are simply singing songs, many are in the middle of an intense competition for territories. For many birds, this struggle could ultimately decide whom they mate with and if they ever raise a family.

When the birds return from their winter feeding grounds, the males usually arrive first. Older, more dominant males will reclaim their old territories: a tree, shrub, or even a window ledge. Younger males will try to challenge the older ones for space by mimicking the song that the older males are singing. The birds that can sing the loudest and the longest usually wind up with the best territories. This is important because the males with the good territories will attract the most females and stand the best chance of mating.

away. With their calls, the monkeys are alerting others that they have claimed a territory and are prepared to defend it. It turns out that each troop of howler monkeys has its own unique call. Scientists believe that these calls contain information on the size of the troop and the status of the dominant males.

CALLING FOR A MATE

One important use of sound in the animal kingdom centers on the act of mating. Visual and chemical signals are important, too, but many times it's a simple call or song that gets the mating process rolling. Mating calls are used by a whole host of animals. From the smallest crickets and frogs to giants, such as elephants and moose, animals use a variety of sounds to alert potential partners that the time is right. Most often, the male of the species makes the first call. His call means something like,

CRICKET THERMOMETERS

One of the most fascinating facts about crickets is how their chirps are related to the outdoor temperature. As the air temperature rises, the rate at which crickets chirp also rises. In the case of the snowy tree cricket, this relationship is so predictable that naturalists rely on these insects as living thermometers.

According to *The Old Farmer's Almanac,* if you want to calculate the outdoor temperature in degrees Fahrenheit, count how many times a cricket chirps in 14 seconds and add 40. So, for example, if a cricket chirps 22 times in 14 seconds, the temperature is about 62° F (22 + 40 = 62). To calculate the temperature in degrees Celsius, the formula is a bit more complicated. First, count the chirps for 25 seconds. Divide that number by 3 and add 4. According to this formula, if a cricket chirps 45 times in 25 seconds, the temperature is 19° C (45 ÷ 3= 15 + 4 = 19).

At first, many people believed that this idea was nothing more than an old folk legend. As scientists studied the relationship, however, they agreed that it was real. Although this method is scientifically accurate, it is not always easy to use cricket chirps to tell the temperature. One big problem is trying to count the chirps from a single cricket. On a warm spring night, when crickets are mating, there can be hundreds of crickets chirping all around you. Trying to focus on the sound produced by a single cricket is a little like trying to listen to a single voice in a 100-person choir. With practice, however, it can be done. So, the next time you are on a camping trip and you are wondering what the temperature is, you might just want to listen to the crickets.

The chirping noise that a cricket makes is actually the sound of its wings brushing together, usually during a mating call.

"Here I am. Come over, check me out and compare me to the other guys."

When a female hears the call, she will seek out the source of the sound and check out the male. Females select the males that are most fit to mate. They use the loudness and duration of the calls to help them judge how fit a male is. In the animal world, the general rule of thumb is that stronger males will have louder and longer calls. Once the female decides upon a partner, she'll usually respond with either a visual signal or a sound of her own. Then, the mating can begin.

Unless you live in the center of a city, you can hear the mating calls of crickets on almost any spring or summer evening. Crickets make their unusual chirping sound by rubbing their wings together. The left wing has anywhere from 50 to 250 comb-like teeth on it. The cricket rubs this wing against the right wing, which has an area that looks kind of like the end of an ice scraper. The pitch of the chirp depends on how many teeth are rubbing against the scraper and how fast the wings are being rubbed together. Most cricket chirps are between 1,500 Hz and 10,000 Hz. Larger cricket make lower sounds. Large or small, crickets tend to chirp more when the temperatures rise.

To human ears, all cricket chirps sound pretty much the same. Yet, scientists have discovered that most species have three distinct calls. The first is the "calling chirp," designed to attract females. Once a female shows interest, the male will use the "courtship chirp." This stimulates the female to mate. If another male cricket moves in on the first male, the first male will give off a "fighting chirp." Different species of crickets have their own distinctive chirps.

Another call with which many people are familiar is the mating croak of male frogs. Each species has its own mating call, but

A male bullfrog croaks with a loud, distinct mating call.

EAVESDROPPING FOR DINNER

Listening to other people's conversations is considered rude. However, in the rest of the animal kingdom, it could lead to a midnight snack. Many predators use the mating calls of other animals to help them home in on their favorite prey. In the tropics, bats are particularly good at picking up on the mating call of male tree frogs. As a defense, some frogs will shorten their calls, which makes them more difficult to find. Unfortunately, this also makes the male less desirable to a female frog.

In some cases, a group of males croak together at the same time. With so many signals coming from different directions, the bat may have problems zeroing in on a specific frog. Other frogs will take the stealth approach. They will sit silently near a good croaker and hope that he attracts both a predator and a mate. When the predator eats the more vocal male, the silent one moves in and mates with the female.

the call of the bullfrog really stands out. Like crickets, male bullfrogs start their serenade at dusk. Once they get going, the sound can be deafening, especially for people camping near a pond or stream. Before bullfrogs start croaking, they seek out the best calling sites. These usually are along the edge of a pond, where there is plenty of still water.

Frogs make their croaks by inflating a large, balloon-like sac on their throats. This sac acts like a resonating chamber and makes the sound very deep. In general, the frogs with the deepest croaks are the largest, strongest males. When a female hears a croak, she can usually tell how big the "croaker" is. Often, smaller frogs will lurk in the water near a large croaking male; when a female comes by to mate, they sneak in and grab her first. Staying on the outskirts of the water has another advantage for smaller frogs. Sometimes the croak of a frog will attract not only a mate, but also a predator.

ANIMAL LOVE SONGS

Many animals use simple calls to attract a mate, but songbirds have turned the act of serenading a potential suitor into a refined art. Still, our fine-feathered friends aren't the only animals that use intricate vocal signals to attract a mate. In fact, some have even had their songs turned into hit records. The reason that humans aren't familiar with these other caroling creatures is that most live under water.

As it turns out, many species of fish and marine mammals "sing" to attract mates. In the Pacific Ocean off the coast of Washington State lives a fish called a midshipman. Like many species of fish, midshipman males build nests with their tails in tidal pools along the shore. Once a nest is built, the midshipman will "sing" to attract a female. If the female finds him desirable, she will lay her eggs in the nest and he will fertilize them. After fertilizing the first set of eggs, the male will sing again, trying to attract more females. A good vocalist can fill his nest with several thousand eggs from as many as a dozen different females.

When a midshipman sings, he makes a low-frequency hum that can be picked up more than a mile away. As with birds, females are attracted to the males that sing the longest and strongest. It also appears that females prefer males that sing the lowest-frequency songs. Scientists discovered this by doing a series of tests called playback studies. They used underwater microphones called **hydrophones** to record the songs of different males. By playing the songs back through a speaker, they were able to see which songs attracted the most females.

Underwater recording has become commonplace among researchers who study animal communication. However, the technology that helps people do that is very recent. The big breakthrough came in the 1950s, when technicians working for the U.S. Navy accidentally recorded the first whale songs. At the time, the Navy's main objective was to keep track of Soviet submarines. At first, the whale songs were classified, but by the mid-1960s, marine biologist Roger Payne's studies completely changed what people knew about animal communication and whales.

UNLOCKING THE MYSTERY OF WHALE SONGS

For hundreds of years, people have known that humpback whales make sounds. When mariners in the past told about Sirens singing to them at night when they were far out at sea, they were probably hearing humpback whales. However, it was only recently that these sounds were understood to be animal communication. In the mid-1960s, marine biologist Roger Payne used hydrophones to make extensive recordings of humpback whale sounds. After he and several other scientists analyzed the tapes, they made a fascinating discovery.

They discovered that the clicks, whistles, and pops are not random. They follow distinct patterns or themes that repeat continuously, like the phrases of a song. Just like birds, humpback whales sing songs. In fact, they sing some of the longest songs of any creature in the animal kingdom. A single song can last as long as 15 minutes. What's more, the whales are constantly changing their songs and inventing new phrases to go along with common themes that get carried over from one year to the next.

There are still many questions about why humpback whales sing. Most marine scientists believe that at least part of it has to do with mating. Whales that sing the longest and strongest songs tend to be the older, more dominant males. Some scientists also believe that whale songs allow the males to keep their distance from one another and to establish a hierarchy within a local group.

Whether they are singing for love or singing to show their dominance, humpback whale songs may have helped save the species from extinction. For hundreds of years, humans hunted humpbacks. When Payne began his research, the number of humpbacks was becoming dangerously low. In 1970, Payne released a record album of his recordings entitled *Songs of the Humpback Whale*. Not only was the record a commercial success, but it also alerted the public to what was happening to whales all over the world.

Whale researcher Roger Payne pets a southern right whale in Peninsula Valdez, Argentina. Payne's humpback whale recordings, produced in the 1960s, are world famous.

ROGER PAYNE TAKES THE PLUNGE

For close to half a century, Dr. Roger Payne has been one of the most important people working in the field of marine biology. He may not be as famous as undersea explorer Jacques Cousteau, or as Robert Ballard, who discovered the wreck of the *Titanic,* but his work is as remarkable as theirs. Along with biologist Scott McVay, Payne discovered and decoded the songs of the humpback whales. This groundbreaking work opened the door to the study of other marine mammals and led to their eventual protection.

Payne was not always a man of the sea. He was born in New York in 1935. As a young man, he earned a bachelor's degree from Harvard University and a Ph.D. from Cornell University. At first, he studied the way bats use sound waves to find their prey—a process called echolocation. He also studied the way owls use sound to help them navigate. In 1967, Payne turned his attention from the skies to the seas. He began to study underwater life. It was at that time that he and McVay made their amazing discoveries. During the last 40 years, Payne has led more than 100 expeditions to study whales in their natural habitat.

In 1971, Payne founded an organization called the Ocean Alliance. He continues to serve as its president. This nonprofit group is dedicated to the protection of whales and their environment. The alliance sponsors studies that investigate the many ways that humans affect the animals that live in the sea. Largely because of Payne's work, in 1986, the International Whaling Commission banned most commercial whaling in the world's oceans.

Inspired by his work, animal activists fought to get restrictions on whaling. Thanks to all of them, humpbacks, as well as other whales, may be singing their songs for many years to come.

ANIMAL INSTRUMENTALISTS

When it comes to using sound for communication, not all animals are vocalists. Some have developed a talent for using other body parts. When one body part is rubbed against another to make a sound, the process is called **stridulation.** Insects and birds both use this technique.

For some animals, tails are useful for making sounds. When beavers are alarmed, they slap their large flat tails against the water. This alerts other beavers to danger.

Rattlesnakes also use their tails to communicate. Like most snakes, when rattlesnakes grow, they shed their skin. In young rattlesnakes, the last scale on the end of the tail doesn't shed. It stays attached to the snake's body by a cord-like structure. Each time the snake sheds its skin, the last scale doesn't shed. As the snake grows, these scales build up. When a rattlesnake feels threatened, it shakes its tail and the scales make a rattling sound.

Some animals make sound by striking other objects with parts of their own bodies. When a woodpecker uses its bill to drill into a tree, it is sometimes doing more than looking for food. It could be courting a mate or warning other male woodpeckers to stay out of its territory. When elephants are annoyed, they stamp their feet. When male gorillas want to establish a hierarchy in their group, they pound on their chests with their fists. This creates a thunderous sound that echoes through the forest. All of this proves that voices are the most effective means of communication for all animals.

Communication Using Touch

MAKING A SOUND requires vibration. Yet, not all vibrations produce sounds that animals can hear. Some sounds are so low or so slow that they are felt instead of heard. Visual signals, chemical scents, and sounds may be the main ways that animals communicate. However, many creatures also use the sense of touch.

Sometimes it's difficult to tell where one sense ends and another begins. When elephants use infrasound to communicate with each other, scientists question if they are hearing the sound or feeling the vibrations. When some garden spiders court females, they often perform dances on the females' webs. The dance looks like a visual display, but it also vibrates the web. Some scientists believe that the vibrations are the male's way of telling the female that he is not a potential meal.

All sorts of communication takes place in a honeybee hive. Scout honeybees perform a dance to tell other members of the hive where to find food. Because it is dark in the hive, other worker bees sometimes get the message by feeling the motion of the scout bees as they do their dances. When a queen bee wants to alert members of the hive, she will release different pheromones. Yet, because a honeybee colony can have more

Bees often rely on touch to get across their messages. When a Queen bee releases pheromones in the hive, her "groomer" bees transport them by rubbing their mouths and antennae against the other bees.

than 50,000 worker bees in it, the queen needs a way to transfer her chemical signals quickly throughout the hive. This is usually done by the sense of touch. Worker bees are always cleaning the queen with their tongues. These "groomers" then move out through the hive while rubbing their antennae and mouths against other bees. These bees will then pick up the queen's pheromones.

GETTING GROOMED

Many animals take part in a variety of touching behaviors that are really a form of communication. In primates, touching is one

LOBSTERS IN A LINE

American spiny lobsters really feel the vibrations when they migrate every fall. When they move south to warmer waters, hundreds of lobsters will slowly follow one another in a line across the ocean floor. One lobster will rest its claws and antennae on the back of the lobster in front of it, making the migrating lobsters look something like a conga line. This group movement keeps all the lobsters moving in the same direction. It also keeps them safe from predators, who tend to back off when they see so many animals together in a group.

American spiny lobsters migrate by walking in a line. This helps keep them safe from predators, who often back away after seeing what looks like a larger single animal.

way that animals comfort each other. In South America, dusky titi monkeys show friendship by sitting next to one another on a tree branch and letting their long tails entwine. Chimpanzees hug each other just like humans. Often, chimps will walk hand in

Chimpanzees communicate through hugs just like humans do. Researchers found that chimps that received hugs after being the victim of another animal's aggressive behavior had less stress than chimps that were not hugged.

GROOMING HELP

"You scratch my back, and I'll scratch yours." Most people have heard this expression before. It usually means, "If you do me a favor, I'll do one for you." Among wild impalas that live on the tick-infested plains of Africa, the expression has a literal meaning. Impalas groom themselves by scraping their coats with their teeth. The teeth act like a comb by removing the ticks from their fur. However, an impala can't reach his or her own neck and head. Impalas must rely on each another for help. When an impala helps a buddy by grooming it, the other animal returns the favor in the exact same way. For example, if one impala uses its teeth to scrape the back of a second impala's neck four times, then the second impala will scrape the first impala exactly four times. The payback is always even.

An African male impala gently grooms another male impala using his teeth.

hand. Finally, although it probably doesn't mean the same thing as it does in humans, chimps also sometimes give each other "high fives."

One of the most common touching behaviors in animals is grooming. Grooming is important for many animals, especially ones that could be affected by ticks and other parasites. House cats and some dogs spend a good deal of time licking themselves. This act is called autogrooming and it helps keep the animal clean.

Allogrooming (or social grooming, as it is often called) is when one animal grooms another animal. Good hygiene is only part of the reason for this type of behavior. Social grooming helps to reinforce the relationships between group members. Social grooming also helps maintain the hierarchy in a group.

KEEPING ORDER AND SAYING SORRY

When animals participate in social grooming, they usually follow a pre-set order according to the hierarchy of the group. Chimpanzee mothers will groom their children. Although sons will occasionally return the favor, it's usually left up to the daughters to take care of their mother. Female chimps will also groom dominant males. In many cases, this helps the female gain the upper hand when it comes time for the males to select a mate. Younger, less dominant male chimps will groom older males with higher social status. This action helps to communicate the fact that the younger males will not threaten the rule of the alpha individuals.

Social grooming also comes into play after two animals have fought. When two high-ranking European mountain sheep battle over social standing or a potential mate, the loser will often groom the winner, licking his head and shoulders. This is a way

PETTING PETS

Whether it's a dog, cat, guinea pig, or horse, most pets (with the exception of goldfish, perhaps) enjoy a rub on the head and a scratch behind the ear. The reason that our animal friends enjoy petting so much is that the act of petting is really a form of grooming. Not only does it relax them, but it also allows them to bond with the human who's doing the petting. When you pet an animal, you are communicating that you are not a threat and that they are welcome in the territory that they share with you. To show their appreciation, many dogs will lick the person petting them. This is their way of returning the favor.

of saying, "I'm sorry for challenging you, and now I know my position."

Male-to-male grooming also plays a role in helping individuals set up their own territories. During mating season, white-tailed deer bucks often will groom one another on the forehead and under the tail. These are the locations of the main male scent glands. Some scientists believe that this special type of grooming allows the males to learn one another's scents. Then, when they are in search of a mate, they will know when they cross into another male's territory.

SHARING THE LOVE

One of the most important times that animals communicate by touch is when they are preparing to mate. In many groups of animals, grooming and nuzzling is often an important step in the mating process. Many scientists believe that these acts relax the partners and create a sense of trust. For example, most species of parrots are monogamous and usually mate for life. When mates reunite after being separated for a while, they usually begin grooming one another. Some scientists think that this is their way of saying how much they missed each other. By grooming each other, they are getting reacquainted and are building a trust bond before mating again.

Grooming also has a calming effect on impatient males. In troops of monkeys, male-to-male grooming is much more

BUTTING HEADS

Sometimes, despite calming behaviors (such as grooming) and threat displays, conflicts will arise between individuals in the same group and things will get physical. During mating season, fights between male chimps and baboons can be bloody, although they are usually not fatal. Among large **ungulates,** physical confrontations can lead to serious face offs. Moose, deer, elk, and antelope often lock antlers in physical contests that can last for an hour or more. They end when one animal eventually backs off. Perhaps the most spectacular physical confrontations of this kind happen between two mountain sheep.

Weighing in at more than 300 lb (136 kg), mountain sheep rams have large curled horns and thick skulls. They can literally butt heads without causing serious damage. During these lengthy wrestling matches, the rams circle each other and use their heads to crash into the sides of their opponents, trying to knock them over. If that doesn't work, the two rams will charge each other head-on, smashing their skulls together. During mating season, the sounds of these butting battles can echo throughout the mountains for many miles. Although the force of impact is tremendous, the rams don't usually get seriously injured. Eventually, one ram will give up and leave, allowing the victor to mate.

common when females go into estrus. Some researchers believe that the males are trying to calm one another to prevent fights. Because the dominant males mate first, the younger males have to wait their turn. This creates tension in the troop. The male-to-male grooming is like one male telling another, "Be patient, buddy; you'll get your turn someday, too."

In some cases, younger males can move up the social ladder by grooming older males. It earns the younger male "privilege points." Researchers in the field have observed that in many cases after a long grooming session a dominant male will allow a younger male to mate with a female that would normally be off limits.

DANCE OF THE DOLPHINS

Only recently have scientists started to understand just how sophisticated dolphin communication is. Most people know that dolphins are active and intelligent creatures. Leaping in and out of the water and calling loudly, dolphins communicate through both visual displays and sounds. Recently, researchers have discovered that dolphins also rely heavily on the sense of touch to express themselves.

Though they live in the ocean, dolphins are mammals that breathe air and give birth to live young. Female dolphins nurse and care for the young until they are ready to fend for themselves. Dolphins live in large groups, which are usually led by a few dominant males. Communication within a dolphin community is important because they often work as a group to hunt and protect their young.

Dolphin skin, especially the areas around the blowhole, jaw, eyes, fins, tail, and genitals, is very sensitive. Dolphins often are seen rubbing against one another in non-threatening ways.

A bottlenose dolphin communicates through squeaks, whistles, and body language. Since they don't have vocal cords, the sounds are produced using three pairs of air sacs located under the blowhole on top of its head.

Sometimes one dolphin will stroke another with its flippers. When they are swimming in groups, they will often swim next to each other, with one dolphin resting a fin on the dolphin next to it. When dolphins reunite after a separation, they rub their dorsal (top) fins together in a greeting that looks a little like humans shaking hands.

When they are not actively mating, dolphins usually stay with others of their own sex. During mating time, the males become aggressive. If a female dolphin doesn't immediately respond to a male, he will chase her. In some cases, a small group of males will join forces and try to separate one female from a group. They will swim after her for hours while using their snouts to push and poke at her, until she finally mates with one of them.

SHOCKING DEVELOPMENTS

In fresh water streams and rivers of South America, knifefish have an interesting way of using the sense of touch to communicate with members of its own species. Instead of stroking or grooming, knifefish use electricity to communicate. A knifefish generates electricity in a special structure found in its tail. This structure, made of modified nerve and muscle cells, is called an electric organ.

In some species of knifefish, the output of the electric organ is so intense that it is used to stun and kill prey. This is the case in the electric eel, which is not a true eel—it's really a species of knifefish. Electric eels can generate up to 600 volts of electricity, which is enough to stun a horse. Most other species of knifefish generate only a few volts. These weak currents help the fish navigate, find prey, and locate a mate.

Scientists believe that knifefish developed their unique ability because of the environment in which they live. Most knifefish are most active at night. They are usually found in lagoons and shallow ponds, where the water is dark and murky. Because it is difficult for them to see in their surroundings, they rely on **electrolocation** to find their way and locate prey.

The electrolocation system varies among different species of knifefish, but all of the systems basically work the same way. The electric organ generates a field around the fish. When the fish swims near an object or when another fish swims by, the electric field changes. Special electroreceptor cells located near the head and mouth of the knifefish pick up these changes. Then, the fish either steers clear of the object or moves in for the kill.

Each species of knifefish produces its own unique electric current. Because of this, members of the same species can communicate with one another. This is particularly useful when a male knifefish is protecting its territory or looking for a mate. When knifefish mate, the male and female swim in a type of spiral dance, and each fish sends electrical signals to the other. All of this electricity flowing through the water would normally make the couple easy prey for larger electric fish that feed off them. To counteract the threat, some knifefish can change their electrical signal so that an eavesdropping electric eel will miss it entirely.

6

Communicating with Other Animals

IT'S CLEAR THAT animals communicate with one another in many different ways. Through visual signals, sounds, scents, and touch, most animals have at least one way of sending messages to one another. The big question is whether these messages represent a **language.** Before that question can fully be answered, we must take a look at what a language really is.

In the most general sense, language is defined as communication using a system of arbitrary sounds, written symbols, gestures, or signals that have standard or agreed-upon meanings. When you say or write the word *tree*, people who speak English have a pretty good idea of what you mean. However, what if you were to travel to China and use the word *tree* there? Unless the person you were speaking to spoke English, they would not know that you were speaking about a living thing that grows in the ground. In Chinese, there are different sounds and written symbols for the word *tree*. This is what we mean when we say that language uses arbitrary sounds and symbols. Words by themselves have no real meaning.

In order to understand what is being written or said, you first have to know what each of the sounds or symbols means. There are thousands of languages in the world, each with its own set of symbols and sounds used to describe the world around us.

A second important part of language is that once certain symbols and sounds have been agreed upon, they can be put together in many different ways. We can use the words *dog* and *tree* in different ways. We can say, "The dog hid behind the tree," or "The tree fell on the dog." We use the same words but the expressions have different meanings.

A third point about language is that it allows people to describe places and events that they cannot see. Humans can describe things that are located in distant places, or events that have happened in the past. People also can talk about things that might happen in the future.

Finally, and perhaps most importantly, language has to be learned. In some cases, you learn a language just by listening to those around you. (Just think of all those words that you are not supposed to use, but learned by listening to other people while you were growing up.) In either case, a true language is one that is passed from one generation to the next.

ELEMENTS OF ANIMAL LANGUAGE

Now that we have some understanding of how language works, we can go back and try and answer the question of whether any animals have a true language. According to many leading scientists in the field, the answer is: maybe. Most scientists agree that human language is clearly the most complex, and that no other animal has a communication system that comes close. Many forms of animal communication do have some of the elements of human language. Some scientists believe that certain animals, such as primates and marine mammals, do use a type of language.

For example, vervet monkeys have different sounds for different predators. When an alarm call is given, the monkeys know whether they should be on the lookout for an eagle, leopard, or snake. These monkeys are using arbitrary sounds that have agreed-upon meanings. This is a key element of language.

A second important point is that the monkeys aren't born knowing the meaning of each of these sounds. Young monkeys learn the meaning of the sounds from listening and watching older monkeys. This learning takes some time. After young monkeys learn the alarm call for seeing an eagle, they use it whenever they see a large bird, even if the bird is harmless. Only after much trial and error do they realize that the eagle call is to be used only for eagles.

Vervet language has many limits. This is why some scientists don't consider it to be a true language. Vervet monkeys don't seem to be able to string different sounds together to make different meanings. For example, a monkey can warn the troop about a snake or eagle being nearby, but it can't use those sounds to say, "The eagle ate a snake." Also, vervets only seem to be able use their language for an immediate threat.

Monkeys aren't the only land mammals that have a complex communication system with elements of human language in it. In the American Southwest, several species of prairie dog have different alarm calls for different predators. Unlike the vervets, though, the prairie dogs can take their communication one step further. Besides communicating the type of predator, the alarm calls also describe the predator's size, where it is going, and how fast it is moving.

Prairie dogs not only have different alarm sounds to alert each other against various predators, but the alarm sounds also communicate the predator's size, where it is going, and how fast it is moving.

Dr. Con Slobodchikoff of Northern Arizona University, Flagstaff, conducted much of this groundbreaking research. After studying videotape of prairie dogs in the wild, Dr. Slobodchikoff

LEARNING THEIR SONGS

Even if most animals don't have a true language, many species communicate using sounds that they learn at a young age. This process is called vocal learning. It's especially important for young birds that need to develop their own songs for staking claim to their territory and calling for a mate. When birds first hatch, they can make basic sounds, including chirps and whistles. Scientists say these sounds are innate, meaning that the birds are born with the ability to make them. Most scientists originally believed that the songs that birds sing are innate, too. Yet, this is not entirely true.

Much of the credit for this discovery goes to scientist Peter Marler, who was a professor at the University of California, Davis. He noticed that songbirds of the same species often had slightly different songs, depending on where they were located. He called these differences "song dialects," because they are similar to language dialects in humans. Compare the speech of a person raised in Texas to that of a person raised in Maine. They both speak English, but they sound different. That's because they have different dialects.

To Marler, song dialects didn't make sense. If songs were pre-programmed into the birds' brains at birth, then all the birds of one species should sound the same, no matter where they lived. Learning was the only way that he could explain song dialects. The young birds had to be learning their songs from adults. Working with white-crowned sparrows, Marler showed that baby chicks could produce full songs only if they could hear the songs of adult birds. If the chicks were kept away from adult birds, they would produce abnormal songs as adults. "A songbird, like a child, must learn from others if it is to vocalize normally," Marler wrote.

could match animal calls to different animal reactions. He could also see the predator that the prairie dogs were calling about. Using a sonogram, he isolated the different sounds used in the alarm code.

The real clincher came when he played back recordings of different alarm calls for the prairie dogs. Their reactions showed that they clearly understood what the different sounds meant and where to look for trouble.

DOLPHIN SPEAK

While many scientists believe that animals (even vervet monkeys and prairie dogs) come up a little short of having a true language, the jury is still out when it comes to marine mammals, such as dolphins and killer whales. Like humans, these animals are extremely intelligent and can learn many things. Because they live in the ocean, these creatures are difficult to study. Yet, studies done on captive animals have convinced some scientists that they have a true language and that it's only a matter of time before humans "crack the code."

Dolphins are masters at using sound. They use sound waves to help them navigate and find food by a process called **echolocation.** This system works the same way as SONAR in a submarine. Kenneth Norris, a pioneer in dolphin communication research, discovered dolphin echolocation in the early 1950s.

To use echolocation, a dolphin sends out a series of high-frequency sound waves from a structure on the top of its head called a melon. These waves move through the water and bounce off objects. The reflected waves then return to the dolphin, where they are processed by the animal's inner ear. Depending on how fast the waves return, the dolphin can get a sense of how far away an object is and how big it is.

In the wild, dolphins live in groups called pods. Quite often, many pods will swim together in giant herds that have hundreds or even thousands of dolphins in them. Scientists believe that dolphins in these herds stay in contact with one another by using their echolocation. Using a group of air sacs below its blowhole, a dolphin can produce whistles, pops, and grunts. Recordings suggest that captive dolphins use sounds to form long-term relationships.

Except during mating times and when they are very young, male dolphins generally swim with other males, and females

Mother dolphins stay close to their young calves. If they are separated, the mother and her young will whistle back and forth until they find each other.

swim with females. Mothers form a strong bond with their young, staying near them and swimming with them for several years. During this time, the mothers train their young on how to hunt using echolocation. Mothers also teach youngsters their "signature" whistle.

A signature whistle is like a dolphin's name. When a dolphin calf is born, the mother begins to whistle the same set of sounds over and over again. Eventually, the calf will begin to mimic this whistle. Later, when the young dolphin strays from its mother, she uses the signature whistle to call the baby back to her. In other words, the mother is calling her child's name. Once a dolphin has learned its signature whistle, it keeps it for life. When groups of dolphins come together, they use their signature whistles; it's almost like people introducing themselves to one another at a party.

Dolphins learn many other vocalizations when they are young. These complex sounds, along with motions (such as the classic tail slap), allow dolphins to communicate with one another for hunting, mating, and defending themselves. It's the closest thing in the animal kingdom to a true language—and at least one scientist staked his career on trying to prove it.

JOHN LILLY AND THE DAY OF THE DOLPHIN

Dr. John C. Lilly is perhaps the most famous and controversial figure in the research of dolphin communication systems. Born in 1915, Lilly attended the California Institute of Technology, Pasadena, and Dartmouth Medical School in Hanover, New Hampshire. He received his M.D. from the University of Pennsylvania, but instead of practicing medicine, he began conducting research.

In the early 1950s, Lilly was working for the National Institutes of Health, where he had become an expert in the structure and function of the human brain. It was here that he invented a device to measure brain waves in animals. He also developed an "isolation tank." This was a tank of very salty water maintained at the same temperature as the human body. Floating in the tank allowed him to "free his mind" and made him wonder if marine mammals' brain might gain the same benefit.

In the late 1950s, Lilly left the National Institutes of Health to concentrate on dolphin research. He became convinced that dolphins were using sounds to communicate with each other in a complex language. Using recordings and computers, he began breaking down this language in hopes of decoding it enough to communicate with dolphins. He even went as far as to build a house that he and his wife shared with dolphins. The house had several rooms, but part of it was built under water, allowing the dolphins to interact with humans.

Lilly published dozens of papers on his research with dolphins. Unfortunately, even though he believed that he could communicate with the animals, other scientists had a hard time duplicating his results. Lilly failed to convince the rest of the scientific community that the dolphins were doing anything more than complicated "tricks." Lilly died in 2001. Although much of his research is still being evaluated, he did a tremendous amount to raise human awareness about the intelligence of dolphins and other marine mammals. Also, based partly on his work, Congress passed the Marine Mammal Protection Act of 1972. In his career, Lilly published 19 books. Two films were made about him: *The Day of the Dolphin* and *Altered States*.

CALLING DR. DOLITTLE

Most people have heard about Dr. Dolittle. This fictional character, created by author Hugh Lofting in the 1920s and recently

Though Wilhelm von Osten was not aware of it, it was his slight body motion and change in voice tone that caused the horse Clever Hans to answer his math questions correctly—not the direct animal-human communication he had been hoping for.

portrayed in a series of movies starring Eddie Murphy, can talk to animals. Although it may be quite some time before people get as good at animal communication as Dr. Dolittle, the idea of communicating with other species is not as far-fetched as it may seem. Most dog and cat owners can sense their pets' needs and wants. Grooms and trainers often seem to communicate with horses. People who own parrots carry on conversations with their birds on a regular basis.

Long before John Lilly began his experiments with dolphins, people were trying to communicate with animals. One of the most famous experiments featured a horse named Clever Hans. Hans and his owner, Wilhelm von Osten, lived in Germany in the early 1900s. Von Osten was a retired teacher who believed that many animals were quite intelligent. To prove his point, he spent a great deal of time trying to teach basic math skills to different animals, including his cat, a bear, and Hans, his Arabian stallion. Though von Osten had no success with the cat and the bear, Hans did show promise.

Von Osten "taught" Hans how to do arithmetic. The horse gave his answers by tapping his hoof. As the lessons continued, von Osten branched out. Hans was soon answering questions about music composers and was even able to tell time. Hans would give his answers by either stomping his foot or shaking his head, and he was almost always correct.

As you might expect, von Osten and Hans soon became quite famous. The two traveled around Germany, giving public shows. In 1904, Carl Stumpf, the director of the Berlin Psychological Institute, put together a panel of scientists and other professionals to test Hans. Stumpf was convinced that Hans was not really showing superior intelligence. He believed that somehow the horse was getting signals from von Osten about which answer was correct. After conducting several trials, the members of the committee were convinced that Hans' abilities were real. Stumpf wanted further proof, so he asked one of his students, Oskar Pfungst, to continue the tests. After several more days, Pfungst figured out what was happening.

As it turns out, Clever Hans wasn't so clever after all. Although the horse was intelligent, he didn't really know math from music. What he did have was the ability to sense slight

KANZI THE BONOBO

Despite the setbacks faced by Herbert Terrace, John Lilly and Allen and Beatrice Gardner, researchers continued designing experiments in hopes of communicating with animals. One of the most exciting developments involved a bonobo chimp named Kanzi. Working at the Language Research Center at Georgia State University, Dr. Sue Savage-Rumbaugh taught Kanzi to "speak" using a special computer. Instead of letters, the computer's keyboard had symbols on it that stood for different words.

The fact that Kanzi learned to use the computer came as a shock to his trainers. When he was only six months old, Kanzi came to the language center with his mother, Matata. Researchers spent almost two years working with Matata, trying to teach her how to use the keyboard. They did not have much success. Most of the time, Kanzi was simply "hanging out" with his mother during her lessons. He was not part of the experiments.

Eventually, Matata and Kanzi were separated. Kanzi stayed at the language center and Matata was sent elsewhere. After a few days, Kanzi surprised everyone when he started using the keyboard to display symbols of different objects. He had learned to use the keyboard in the same way that young children learn language: by gradually absorbing the information over time.

changes in von Osten's voice and body language. After von Osten would ask Hans a question, he always made some slight body motion or changed the tone of his voice when he said the correct answer. Hans would sense these changes and respond. The funny thing was that von Osten himself didn't even realize that he was doing it.

Young Kanzi learns to point to symbols on a board in order to communicate. The symbols, called lexigrams, represent words.

Once researchers actively started working with Kanzi, they found that he could quickly learn how to put different symbols together in new ways to make phrases. Kanzi used the computer to create more than 650 different sentences, many using proper grammar. Researchers at the language center were certain that Kanzi was truly speaking to them, although other scientists still are not convinced. The argument may never be settled, but that's part of the fun and intrigue of science.

Though it's been about 100 years since scientists learned their lesson from Clever Hans, researchers are still having problems when it comes to figuring out how to test animal-human communication. In the 1970s, Columbia University psychology professor Herbert Terrace thought he had made a breakthrough.

Dr. Terrace had been reviewing work done with chimps in the 1960s by Allen and Beatrice Gardner. Despite what is shown in movies such as *Planet of the Apes*, chimps and other primates cannot speak. It is physically impossible for them to speak words because they do not have the same vocal structures as humans. However, chimps can make the same hand movements as humans. For this reason, the Gardners decided to teach the chimps American Sign Language. This is the standard form of sign language taught in the United States.

The Gardners worked with a chimp named Washoe. She quickly learned the signs for about 30 different objects. Washoe even started putting several signs together to make short phrases with the words *I* and *you* in them. Dr. Terrace was convinced that Washoe was just mimicking the Gardners and not communicating her own thoughts and feelings. He decided to conduct his own tests.

In 1973, he began working with a chimp that he named Nim Chimpsky in honor of Noam Chomsky, a distinguished professor and expert on the development of language at MIT. Nim was nine months old when the research began. Dr. Terrace followed the same approach as the Gardners by using American Sign Language, but his work was much more intensive. Nim learned more than 125 different signs, including nouns, verbs, and adjectives. Like Washoe, Nim began to put different signs together. Dr Terrace videotaped Nim signing 20,000 different "phrases." At first, Dr. Terrace believed that Nim had started using true language—that Nim could understand and create simple sentences with their own meanings. After spending hours reviewing the tapes, however, Dr. Terrace was forced to conclude that Nim really didn't understand what he was signing. He was simply using the signs to please his trainers and get food rewards.

WHAT WILL THE FUTURE BRING?

Though we have come a long way from the days of Charles Darwin, in many ways, researchers still are just scratching the surface when it comes to understanding animal communication. All the time, researchers conduct new experiments using new technology that help to unlock secrets about the nature of animal communication. Imaging devices, such as CAT scans and MRIs, let scientists see the inner workings of animal brains and compare them with human brains.

One of the people on the cutting edge of today's research is Dr. Eugene S. Morton. He specializes in the natural language of mammals and birds. Dr. Morton has developed rules that make it simple to understand animals when they communicate with one anther.

After spending more than 20 years studying the sounds made by different animals, Morton has found that many animals use the same types of sounds to convey the same message. For example, if an animal is angry and about to attack, the sound that it usually makes will be harsh and have a low frequency. Though they make different sounds, an unfriendly dog growls, an angry bird squawks, and an angry squirrel chatters with the same type of tone. If an animal makes a high-pitched whine, it is usually afraid and is being submissive. Dr. Morton has found a relationship between the tone of an animal sound and the animal's state of mind. Listen to the conversations between people on the street and you'll notice this same conclusion can be made for human communication.

It seems that the more humans discover about animal communication, the more we learn about our own methods of communication. Human language seems much more sophisticated than the communication of a chimpanzee or a barn swallow. Yet, a growing number of researchers are surprised to find out just how similar it is.

Maybe some day humans may be able to talk to the animals like Dr. Dolittle. In the meantime, there are a great many people studying animal communication who are content to eavesdrop on animal "conversations" and try to learn what the animals have to say.

Glossary

bioluminescence   the ability of an animal to make and use light

controlled experiment   an experiment where all the variables are kept the same except the one being tested

courting ritual   a behavior done by an animal while finding a mate

echolocation   an animal navigation system that uses sound waves to estimate the size of objects and their distance from an animal

electrolocation   a system used in some fish to navigate and locate prey

estrus   the time period where a female animal is fertile and ready to mate

ethology   the science that studies animal behavior and communication

experimental psychologist   a scientist who studies animal behavior by doing controlled experiments in the lab or field

Hertz (Hz)   the frequency of a vibration; one Hz equals one vibration per second

hierarchy   a social order within a group of animals

instinct   a behavior that an animal inherits rather than learns

intention movement   a signal to a group of animals that it's time to take a certain action

mating display   a form of nonverbal communication used by animals to attract a mate

monogamous   having only one mate or partner

neurobiology   the science that looks at the detailed structure of the brain and nervous system of different animals

non-verbal communication   communication without the use of sounds or words

olfactory system   the system of the body designed to pick up and process smells

primates   the specific order of mammals that includes monkeys, apes, lemurs, and humans

scent marker   a chemical used by an animal to mark its territory

scent post   an object with a chemical scent marker on it

signal   something that an animal does to communicate. Signals can include sounds, motions, scents, or flashes of light.

Siren   creature with the head of a woman and the body of a bird. In Greek mythology. The Sirens lived on an island, and sang to attract captains to wreck their ships on the rocks surrounding the island.

sound wave   a form of vibrations that carries a sound

species   the smallest unit into which all living things are grouped

stridulation   the process of making a sound by rubbing one body part against another

submissive display   a display that an animal will make toward a more dominant animal in a group

territorial   living in a limited area to feed, nest, and mate

territory   the area in which territorial animals will find food, mate, and carry out most other life functions

threat display   an often defensive action that an animal will make when it is in fear of being attacked

ultrasound   sound with a frequency above 20,000 Hz

ungulate   an animal that has hooves

vertebrate   an animal that has a backbone

Bibliography

Barre, Michael. *Animal Relationships*. Milwaukee: Gareth Stevens Publishing, 1998.

Clutton-Brock, Juliet and Wilson, Don, editorial consultants. *Smithsonian Handbook of Mammals*. New York: DK Publishing, 2002.

Cooke, Fred; Hugh Dingle; Stephen Hutchinson; George McKay; Richard Schodde; Noel Tait; and Richard Vogt. *The Encyclopedia of Animals*. Berkeley, Calif.: University of California Press, 2004.

Doig, Fiona, editor. *Whales, Dolphins and Porpoises*. Pleasantville, N.Y.: Reader's Digest, 1997.

Editors, *Animal Marvels, Communicating*. Milwaukee: Gareth Stevens Publishing, 2001.

Friend, Tim. *Animal Talk, Breaking the Codes of Animal Language*. New York: Free Press, 2004.

Halliday, Tim, editor. *Animal Behavior*. Norman, Okla: University of Oklahoma Press, 1994.

Masson, Jeffery and Susan McCarthy. *When Elephants Weep: The Emotional Lives of Animals*. New York: Delacorte Press, 1995.

Morton, Eugene and Jake Page. *Animal Talk, Science and the Voices of Nature*. New York: Random House, 1992.

Steiger, Sherry and Brad Steiger. *Mysteries of Animal Intelligence*. New York: Tor Books, 1995.

Tomecek, Steve. *Sound: Teachers A-Z Resource Guide*. Bethesda, Md: Discovery Communications, 2000.

Wyatt, Tristram. *Pheromones and Animal Behaviour*. New York: Cambridge University Press, 2003.

Further Resources

BOOKS

Animal Marvels, Communicating. Milwaukee: Gareth Stevens Publishing, 2001.

Clutton-Brock, Juliet and Don Wilson, editorial consultants. *Smithsonian Handbook of Mammals.* New York: DK Publishing, 2002.

Cooke, Fred; Hugh Dingle; Stephen Hutchinson; George McKay; Richard Schodde; Noel Tait; and Richard Vogt. *The Encyclopedia of Animals.* Berkeley, Calif.: University of California Press, 2004.

Dor, Galia. *Dolphins, Their Natural History, Behavior and Unique Relationship with Human Beings.* Hod Hasharon, Israel: Astrolog Publishing, 2004.

Friend, Tim. *Animal Talk, Breaking the Codes of Animal Language.* New York: Free Press, 2004.

Myers, Phillip. *Mammals: An Explore Your World Handbook.* New York: Discovery Books, 2000.

Wyatt, Tristram. *Pheromones and Animal Behaviour.* New York: Cambridge University Press, 2003.

WEB SITES

National Geographic News
http://news.nationalgeographic.com/news/index.html
This site provides news about current discoveries with animals, earth science, and the environment.

Bird and Mammal Acoustic Communication Group

http://biology.st-andrews.ac.uk/bmac/index.htm

This site gives information on some of the latest discoveries in bird and mammal communication by the scientists who are doing the research.

The Cetacean Nation

www.cetacean-nation.com

This site is run by the organization started by John Lilly to spread the latest information about dolphins and other cetaceans.

MarineBio

http://marinebio.org

This site gives detailed information on many creatures that live in the ocean including their habitats and habits.

Picture Credits

Index

About the Author

Stephen M. Tomecek is a geologist and author of more than 40 nonfiction books for both children and teachers. He works as a consultant and writer for The National Geographic Society and Scholastic Inc. Tomecek was the writer and host of the Emmy Award-winning television series *Dr. Dad's Phantastic Physical Phenomena*. He is also the author of the Chelsea House book series *Experimenting with Everyday Science*.